T0083165

HARK, HARK, THE LARK

8 Shakespeare settings for upper voices

Compiled and edited by Bob Chilcott

MUSIC DEPARTMENT

OXFORD
UNIVERSITY PRESS

OXFORD
UNIVERSITY PRESS

Great Clarendon Street, Oxford OX2 6DP,
United Kingdom

Oxford University Press is a department of the University of Oxford.
It furthers the University's objective of excellence in research, scholarship,
and education by publishing worldwide. Oxford is a registered trade mark of
Oxford University Press in the UK and in certain other countries

© Oxford University Press 2015

Bob Chilcott has asserted his right under the Copyright, Designs
and Patents Act, 1988, to be identified as the Editor of this anthology

Each composer has asserted his/her right under the Copyright, Designs and
Patents Act, 1988, to be identified as the Composer/Arranger of their Work(s)

Database right Oxford University Press (maker)

First published 2015

Impression: 2

All rights reserved. No part of this publication may be reproduced,
stored in a retrieval system, or transmitted, in any form or by any means,
without the prior permission in writing of Oxford University Press

Permission to perform the works in this anthology in public
(except in the course of divine worship) should normally be obtained
from the Performing Right Society Ltd (PRS) at www.prsformusic.com
or a local performing right licensing organization, unless the owner or the
occupier of the premises being used already holds a licence from such an
organization. Likewise, permission to make and exploit a recording must
be obtained in advance from the Mechanical-Copyright Protection
Society Ltd (MCPS) at www.prsformusic.com or a local mechanical
copyright licensing organization

Enquiries concerning reproduction outside the scope of the above should be
directed to the Music Rights Department, Oxford University Press, at
music.permissions.uk@oup.com or at the address above

ISBN 978-0-19-340615-5

Music and text origination by
Katie Johnston
Printed in Great Britain on acid-free paper by
Halstan & Co. Ltd, Amersham, Bucks.

Preface

In order to mark the four hundredth anniversary of the death of William Shakespeare, we have collected together eight newly composed settings of some of his most familiar words. Many singers all over the world will be familiar with so many of the songs in Shakespeare's plays through the work of composers such as Ralph Vaughan Williams, Gerald Finzi, Sir Michael Tippett, Frank Martin, and John Rutter, to name but a few. For this collection we have asked composers from Britain, Canada, the United States, Australia, and Finland to put their own stamp on Shakespeare's songs and texts—words that abound with energy and that have so much singing line and rhythm within them; words that, in fact, are in most cases surely meant to be sung.

Our source for the texts, and for general reference, has been The Oxford Shakespeare edition, and we have been extremely lucky to have had guidance from Carol Rutter, Professor of Shakespeare and Performance Studies at Warwick University. I would also like to thank Philip Croydon, Commissioning Editor at Oxford University Press, for his support and guidance on this book, and also Robyn Elton and Laura Jones for their careful editing work.

In putting this collection together, I hope we have achieved our aim of creating a practical performance edition that can be used by choirs everywhere to celebrate the life and work of one of our greatest writers—as well as the music of some wonderful contemporary composers.

Bob Chilcott
June 2015

Also available from Oxford University Press:
Shall I compare thee?: 10 Shakespeare settings for mixed voices (978–0–19–340614–8)

Contents

And will he not come again? 6
Paul Jarman

Blow, blow, thou winter wind 14
Sarah Quartel

Come unto these yellow sands 24
Bob Chilcott

Hark, hark, the lark 30
Alan Bullard

Our revels now are ended 35
Bob Chilcott

Over hill, over dale 40
Andrea Ramsey

When icicles hang by the wall 50
Stephen Hatfield

You spotted snakes with double tongue 58
Jussi Chydenius

And will he not come again?

William Shakespeare
from *Hamlet* (Act 4, Scene 5)

PAUL JARMAN
(b. 1971)

Duration: 3 mins

© Oxford University Press 2015. Photocopying this copyright material is ILLEGAL.

20
Tempo I ♩ = 100
will he not come, and will he not come? And will he not come a-
will he not come a - gain? And will he not come a-
will he not come a - gain? And will he not come a-
Tempo I ♩ = 100
p sempre legato
sim.
con Ped.
26
- gain? No, no, he is dead,
- gain? No, no, he is dead,
- gain? No, no, he is dead,
pp
p
Ped.

32
slightly slower
rall.
pp
Go to thy death - bed, He ne - ver will come a - gain.
Go to thy death-bed, He ne - ver will come a - gain.
Go to thy death-bed, He ne - ver will come a - gain.
slightly slower
rall.
pp

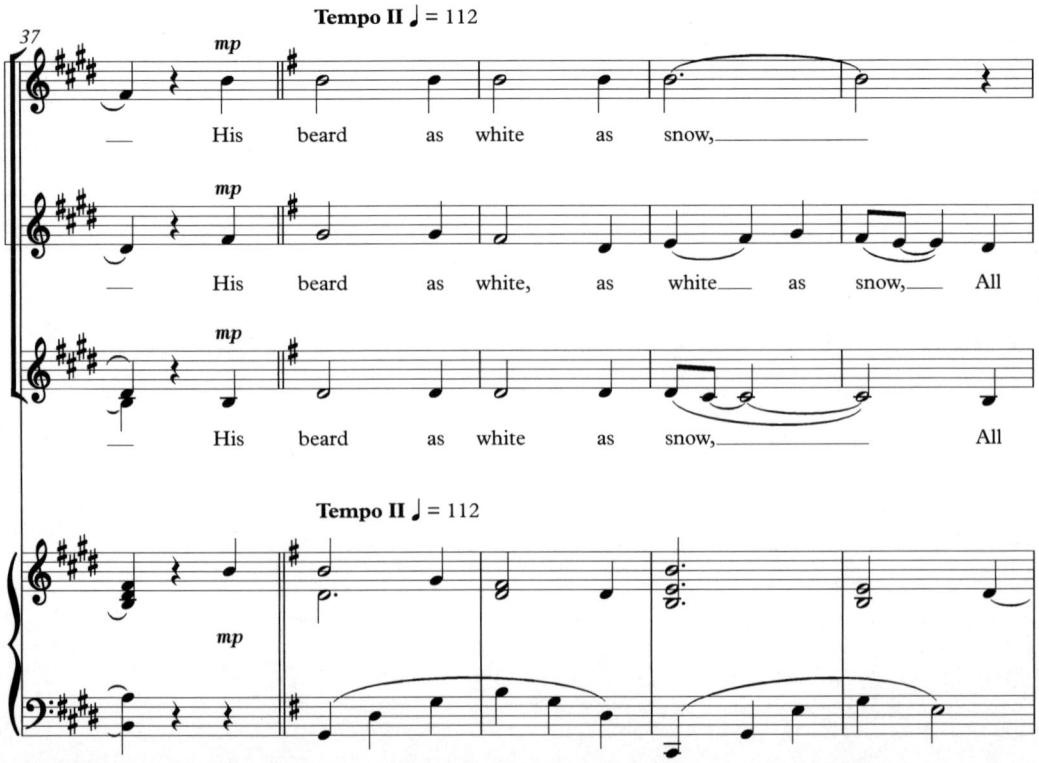
37
Tempo II ♩ = 112
mp
His beard as white as snow,
His beard as white, as white as snow, All
His beard as white as snow, All
Tempo II ♩ = 112
mp

42
poco rall.
slightly slower
pp
All flax - en was his poll.
Gone,
flax - en was his poll.
He is gone,
flax - en was his poll.
Gone,
poco rall.
slightly slower
pp
47
poco accel.
he is gone. He is gone, he is
he is gone. He is gone, he is
he is gone. He is gone, he is
poco accel.

with feeling ♩ = 116
52
p
cresc.
gone. And we cast a-way moan.
p
cresc.
gone. And we cast a-way moan.
p
cresc.
gone. And we cast a-way moan.
with feeling ♩ = 116
p sempre legato
cresc.
57
mp
Mer - cy on his
mp
God have mer - cy on his
mp
God have mer - cy on his
mp

62
mf
soul.
God have mer - cy
soul.
God have mer - cy
soul.
God have mer - cy
mf
Ped.
rall.
Proudly ♩ = 112
66
cresc.
f
on his soul. And
on his soul, on his soul. And
on his soul. And
rall.
Proudly ♩ = 112
cresc.

70
f
will he not come, and will he not come? And will he not come a-
f
will he not come a - gain? And will he not come a-
f
will he not come a - gain? And will he not come a-
f
76
mf
cresc.
f
- gain? No, no, he is dead,
mf
cresc.
f
- gain? No, no, he is dead,
mf
cresc.
f
- gain? No, no, he is dead,
mf
cresc.
f
Ped.

slightly slower
rall.
82
sub. p
mp
mf
Go to thy death - bed, He ne - ver will come a -
Go to thy death - bed, He ne - ver will come a -
Go to thy death - bed, He ne - ver will come a -
slightly slower
rall.
mp
cresc.
mf
molto rall.
86
p
pp
- gain. God have mer - cy on his soul.
- gain. God have mer - cy on his soul.
- gain. God have mer - cy on his soul.
molto rall.
p
pp

Blow, blow, thou winter wind

William Shakespeare
from *As You Like It* (Act 2, Scene 7)

SARAH QUARTEL
(b. 1982)

Duration: 2.5 mins

© Oxford University Press 2015. Photocopying this copyright material is ILLEGAL.

13
mf
blow, thou win - ter wind,
mf
blow, thou win - ter wind,
mf
17
mp
Thou art not so un - kind As
mp
Thou art not so un - kind As
mp
21
mf
man's in - gra - ti - tude.
mf
man's in - gra - ti - tude.
mf

25
Thy tooth is not so keen, Be -
Thy tooth is not so keen, Be -
29
mp
- cause thou art not seen, Al -
mp
- cause thou art not seen, Al -
mp
33
f
- though thy breath be rude.
f
- though thy breath be rude.
f

37
Hey - - ho! sing hey - - ho! un -
Hey - - ho! sing hey - - ho! un -
41
-to the green hol - ly. Most
-to the green hol - ly. Most
45
sub. p
friend - ship is feign - ing, most lov - ing, mere fol - ly. Then
sub. p
friend - ship is feign - ing, most lov - ing, mere fol - ly. Then

49
hey - - ho! the hol - ly! This life, this
hey - - ho! the hol - ly! This life, this
sub. p
mf
54
mf
mp
life is most jol - ly.
mf
mp
life is most jol - ly.
mp
58
unis. mp
Freeze, freeze, thou bit - ter sky,
mp
Freeze, freeze, thou bit - ter sky,
sim.
sim.

63
mf
mp
freeze, thou bit - ter sky, That
mf
mp
freeze, thou bit - ter sky, That
mf
67
dost not bite so nigh As
dost not bite so nigh As
mp
71
mf
be - ne - fits for - got.
mf
be - ne - fits for - got.
mf

75
Though thou the wa - ters warp, Thy
Though thou the wa - ters warp, Thy
79
mp
sting is not so sharp As
mp
sting is not so sharp As
mp
83
f
friend re - mem - bered not.
f
friend re - mem - bered not.
f

87
Hey - ho! sing hey - ho! un - to the
Hey - ho! sing hey - ho! un - to the
92
green hol - ly. Most friend - ship is feign - ing, most
green hol - ly. Most friend - ship is feign - ing, most
97
sub. p
lov - ing, mere fol - ly. Then hey - ho! the hol - ly!
sub. p
lov - ing, mere fol - ly. Then hey - ho! the hol - ly!
sub. p

102
mf
mp
This life, this life is most jol - ly.
This life, this life is most jol - ly.
mf
mp
107
mf
Blow,
Blow,
sim.
111
f
blow,
blow,
blow,
blow,
sim.

115
sub. p
This
sub. p
This
f
119
life, this life is most jol - ly!
life, this life is most jol - ly!
sub. p
mp
124
rit.
rit.

for Cheryl Dupont and the New Orleans Children's Chorus

Come unto these yellow sands

William Shakespeare
from *The Tempest* (Act 1, Scene 2)

BOB CHILCOTT
(b. 1955)

Duration: 1.5 mins

© Oxford University Press 2015. Photocopying this copyright material is ILLEGAL.

* *whist* = into silence

* *featly* = neatly and elegantly
† unpitched; bark like a dog
‡ *burden* = chorus

28
mf
f
-wow! The watch dogs bark, Hark, hark! Bow - wow! The
mf
f
-wow! The watch dogs bark, Hark, hark! Bow - wow! The
mf
f
32
watch dogs bark. Come, come un - to these yel - low
watch dogs bark. Come, come un - to these yel - low
35
sands, And then take hands, Come, come un -
sands, And then take hands, Come, come un -

* *chanticleer* = a domestic cockerel

47
sub. p
S.1
cock a did - dle dow, cock a did - dle
sub. p
S.2
cock a did - dle dow,
sub. p
A.
bow - wow, bow - wow,
sub. p

50
pp
dow, cock a did - dle dow.
pp
cock a did - dle dow, cock a did - dle dow.
pp
bow - wow.
pp

Hark, hark, the lark

William Shakespeare
from *Cymbeline* (Act 2, Scene 3)

ALAN BULLARD
(b. 1947)

Duration: 2 mins

© Oxford University Press 2015. Photocopying this copyright material is ILLEGAL.

* *Phoebus* = Apollo, the sun-god
† *'gins* = begins to

* the bud of a marigold
† *ope* = open

25
f
pret - ty is, my la - dy sweet a - rise, A -
f
is, that pret - ty is, my la - dy sweet a - rise,
f
con Ped.
28
ff
- rise, a - rise!
ff
A - rise, a - rise!
ff
Ped.
31
meno mosso
pp
Hark, hark, the
pp
Hark, hark, the
meno mosso
8va
p
pp

Tempo I (♩ = 100)
35
p
pp
lark!
Hark, hark,
p
p
lark!
Hark,
Tempo I (♩ = 100)
come prima
p
38
mp
(mp)
pp
hark, hark,
hark, hark,
hark, hark!
mf
p
hark, hark, hark, hark, hark!
8va
41
poco rit.
accel.
molto rit.
poco rit.
accel.
molto rit.
(8)
pp
ppp
Ped.

for Angie Johnson and the Young Naperville Singers

Our revels now are ended

William Shakespeare
from *The Tempest* (Act 4, Scene 1)

BOB CHILCOTT
(b. 1955)

Duration: 3 mins

© Oxford University Press 2015. Photocopying this copyright material is ILLEGAL.

11
S.
spir - its, and Are melt-ed in - to air, in - to thin air,
A.
spir - its, and Are melt-ed in - to air, in - to thin air,
14
And, like the base - less fab - ric of this vi - sion, this
And, like the base - less fab - ric of this vi - sion, this
17
mp
vi - sion, The cloud-capped tow'rs,
mp
vi - sion, The cloud-capped tow'rs, the gor - geous
mp

19
the gor - geous pa - la - ces, the great globe, the great
pa - la - ces, The sol - emn tem - ples, the great
21
mf
globe it - self, Yea, all which it in - her - it, shall dis - solve, shall dis -
mf
globe it self, Yea, all which it in - her - it, shall dis - solve, shall dis -
mf
24
mp
- solve, And, like this in - sub - stan - tial pa - geant
mp
- solve, And, like this in - sub - stan - tial pa - geant
mp

* *rack* = cloud or mist driven by the wind
† *on* = of

37
and our lit - tle life Is round - ed with a
and our lit - tle life Is round - ed with a
40
mp
sleep, a sleep, round - ed
mp
sleep, a sleep, round - ed
mp
43
rit.
p
with a sleep.
p
with a sleep.
rit.
p
pp

Over hill, over dale

William Shakespeare
from *A Midsummer Night's Dream* (Act 2, Scene 1)

ANDREA RAMSEY

Duration: 3 mins

* *tho-rough* = through. The standard early modern spelling of the word, indicating pronunciation in two syllables.

© Oxford University Press 2015. Photocopying this copyright material is ILLEGAL.

* *pale* = an area of land enclosed by a wooden fence

19
mp
Swift - er than the moon - ës sphere,
mp
Swift - er than the moon - ës sphere,
p
mp
22
S./A.
unis. mf
And I serve the Fai - ry Queen To
mf
mp
25
dew her orbs u - pon the
mf

* *pensioners* = the title of Queen Elizabeth's royal bodyguard

* *savours* = fragrance

48
f
I must go seek some dew - drops
I must go seek some dew - drops
mf
52
mf
here, And hang a
here, And hang a
mp
55
pearl in ev - 'ry cow - slip's
pearl in ev - 'ry cow - slip's

* *lob* = country bumpkin, clown, or lout

70
S./A.
unis.
rit.
molto rit.
Our Queen and all her elves
come here a -
p
pp
Tempo I ♩ = 120
74
- non.
mp
77
(S./A. unis.)
mf
O - ver hill, o - ver dale,
mp
mf
80
Tho - rough bush, tho - rough bri - - er,

82
O - ver park, o - ver pale,
85
Tho-rough flood, tho-rough fire;
mf
ff
88
S.
f
I do wan - der ev - 'ry - where
A.
f
I do wan - der ev - 'ry - where
mf
dim.
mp

92
mp
Swift - er than the moon - ës sphere,
mp
Swift - er than the moon - ës sphere,
p
mp
95
unis. mf
S./A.
And I serve the Fai - ry Queen
f
To
mf
mp
98
dew her orbs
u - pon the
f
102
green.
ff
f
ff

When icicles hang by the wall

William Shakespeare
from *Love's Labour's Lost* (Act 5, Scene 2)

STEPHEN HATFIELD
(b. 1956)

Duration: 2.5 mins

All stage directions are optional.

© Oxford University Press 2015. This music is published by arrangement with Boosey & Hawkes. Photocopying this copyright material is ILLEGAL.

* *blows his nail* = warms his hands by blowing on them

21
agitato
p
mp
night - ly sings the star - ing owl: 'Tu -
dolce
agitato
p
night - ly sings, night - ly sings the star - ing owl:
dolce
agitato
p
night - ly sings, night - ly sings the star - ing owl:
25
mf
-whit, Tu - whoo! Tu - whit, Tu-whit, Tu - whit, Tu-whoo!
p like an echo
mf
mp
'Tu-whit, Tu - whoo! Tu - whoo! Tu -
p like an echo
mf
mp
'Tu-whit, Tu - whoo! Tu - whoo! Tu -
29
mp
p
Tu - tu - whit, Tu-whoo! Tu - whit!'
p
-whit, Tu - whoo! Tu - whoo! Tu - whit!'
p
-whit, Tu - whoo! Tu - whoo! Tu - whit, Tu-whit, Tu -

* *keel* = to stir the pot and scrape the inner sides to prevent it boiling over

[1] stage direction: 'ha!' indicates that singers should give a rheumy, phlegmy cough
[2] stage direction: 'Marian' blows her nose
* *saw* = sermon

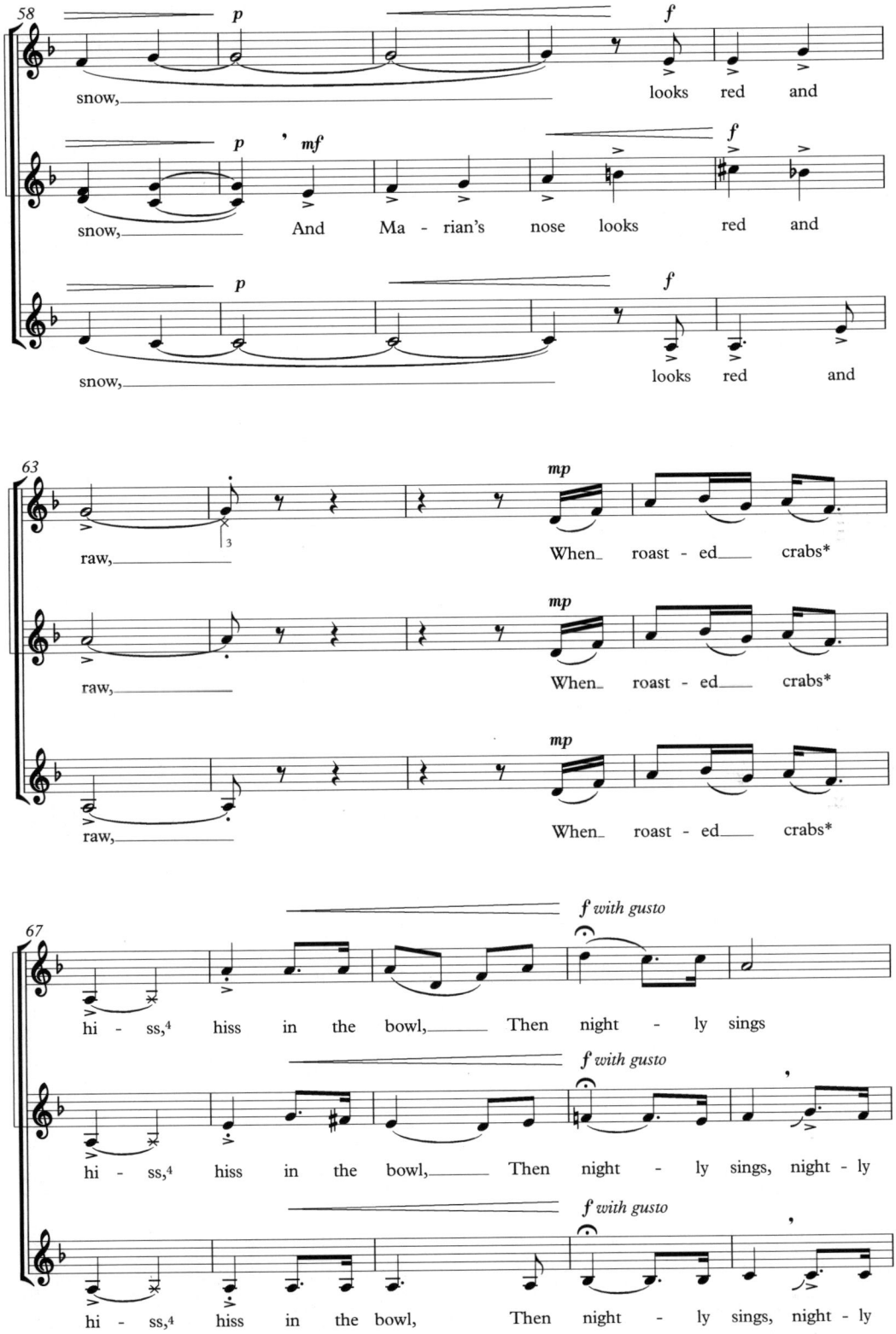

[3] stage direction: 'Marian' gives an even louder honk
[4] stage direction: some or all singers warm their hands over the bowl
* *crabs* = crab-apples

allargando
72
mp
mf
the star - ing owl: 'Tu - whit, Tu - whoo! Tu -
p like an echo
sings the star - ing owl: 'Tu - whit, Tu - whoo! Tu -
p like an echo
sings the star - ing owl: 'Tu - whit, Tu - whoo! Tu -
76
mp
- whit, Tu - whit, Tu - whit, Tu - whoo! Tu - tu - whit, Tu - whoo! Tu -
mf
mp
- whoo! Tu - whit, Tu - whoo! Tu - whoo! Tu -
mf
mp
- whoo! Tu - whit, Tu - whoo! Tu - whoo! Tu -
80
p
mp
- whit!' A mer - ry note,
p
mp
mf
- whit!' A - mer - ry note, a
p
- whit, Tu - whit, Tu - whit, Tu - whoo!'

84
mf
f
a mer - ry note, While greas - y Joan doth keel the
mer - ry note,
mf
f
A mer - ry note, While greas - y Joan doth keel the
88
sub. p
pot, while greas - y Joan doth keel the pot, keel the
p
While greas - y Joan doth keel the pot, keel the
sub. p
pot, while greas - y Joan doth keel the pot, keel the
Meno mosso
'Tu - whit, Tu - whoo!
Tu - whit, Tu - whoo!'
93
div.
mp
(opt. SOLO)
p
pot. 'Tu - whit, Tu - whoo!'
p
mp
p
pot. 'Tu - whit, Tu-whoo! Tu - whit, Tu - whoo!'
mp
p
pot. 'Tu - whit, Tu-whoo!'

You spotted snakes with double tongue

William Shakespeare
from *A Midsummer Night's Dream* (Act 2, Scene 2)

JUSSI CHYDENIUS
(b. 1972)

Duration: 2.5 mins

© Oxford University Press 2015. Photocopying this copyright material is ILLEGAL.

* *Philomel* = a nightingale. Shakespeare references Ovid's *Metamorphosis*, in which the character Philomela is transformed into a nightingale.

33
cresc.
poco accel.
poco rall.
f
Ne-ver harm Nor spell nor charm Come our love - ly la - dy nigh.
cresc.
f
Ne - ver harm, nor charm Come our love - ly la - dy nigh.
cresc.
f
Ne-ver harm Nor spell nor charm Come our love - ly la - dy nigh.
1.
42a
a tempo
mp dolce
poco rall.
So good night with lul - la - by.
mp dolce
So good night with lul - la - by.
mp dolce
So good night with lul - la - by, lul-la- by.
2.
42b
Slower
p dolce
rall.
So good night, with lul - la - by.
p dolce
So good night, with lul - la - by.
p dolce
So good - night with lul - la, lul - la - by.